A TEEN GUIDE TO THE ROSARY

Copyediting by Natalie Tansill.

Designed by Laura Womack.

Special thanks to all those that contributed to this piece in its original form, especially Sister Joseph Andrew Bogdanowicz, Mark Hart, Natalie Tansill, Kristin Bird, and Marilyn Looker.

For more information about Life Teen or to order additional copies, go online to LifeTeen.com or call us at 1-800-809-3902.

TABLE *of* CONTENTS

INTRODUCTION - 4

HISTORY OF THE ROSARY - 7

HOW TO PRAY THE ROSARY - 8

TAKING IT FURTHER:
DIFFERENT WAYS TO PRAY THE ROSARY

PRAYING WITH SCRIPTURE - 16

ONE MINUTE REFLECTIONS:
JOYFUL MYSTERIES - 20
LUMINOUS MYSTERIES - 26
SORROWFUL MYSTERIES - 32
GLORIOUS MYSTERIES - 38

GOING EVEN DEEPER:
JOYFUL MYSTERIES - 45
LUMINOUS MYSTERIES - 55
SORROWFUL MYSTERIES - 67
GLORIOUS MYSTERIES - 76

FREQUENTLY ASKED QUESTIONS - 85

INTRODUCTION

SISTER JOSEPH ANDREW BOGDANOWICZ, OP
DOMINICAN SISTERS OF MARY,
MOTHER OF THE EUCHARIST, ANN ARBOR, MI
www.sistersofmary.org

It was along one of those lone, dark trails that our car sped on a winter night many years ago. Though we had just left my grandparents' home and I could still taste my grandmother's warm apple fritters, I fought an uneasiness in my childlike perception of this "pitch black night." My father showed no fear and his strength helped to calm me in the back seat. Still, I wanted my mom's soft lap, my special place so recently claimed by my infant brother. Mom was singing quietly and I was straining to hear her melody. Suddenly she caught sight of the glimmering quarter-moon and said, "Look! Mother Mary has her window open and she's smiling at you!" As if on a cue only married couples understand, my father began to lead our nightly family Rosary. Gazing upon the moon, I suddenly understood. Each sparkling star represented a "Hail Mary" surrounding Mary's round-window; thus, the sky was filled with the prayers we were offering in our warming-up car! From that moment on, the feel of Rosary beads between my fingers always returns me to our heavenly Mother's warm embrace. I, too, am held within her Rosary.

Years later, as a high school teacher, I made a Rosary to give a grief-stricken non-Catholic student as his father lay dying. "Just hold onto it," I coached him until he could learn how to pray it. "Our heavenly Mother will comfort your fears." Evidently Mary was in it for the long run as seven years later, I received a letter from this now college grad who had landed his first job. In familiar handwriting, he told me: "Sister, you once promised that through the Rosary, Mother Mary would always protect me. You were right; today I owe her my life." He continued: "One icy morning, en route to work, my truck lost traction on the interstate. Instinctively, my hand shot into my pocket to grab my Rosary. The truck jack-knifed and careened wildly into trees. The Rosary fell and instantaneously, I lunged down to grab it just as my truck bolted to a crashing stop. I lay there surprised to be alive…when I felt my face against a tree. I was pinned in the floor space by a tree that had shot through the window, laying claim to the area wherein my head and chest had just been. Trembling, I began praying my Rosary…Mary had saved my life."

Today, as a Professed Dominican Sister, I am blessed to wear what I consider to be the most beautiful Religious habit in the Church! Though I love the long folds of white material and the starkness of the black veil, it will always be the long 15-decade Rosary that I carry at my side that most has my heart. Church tradition tells us that St. Dominic received the Rosary from Mother Mary when he was in his own darkness… trying to bring the Light of Truth to unresponsive people who had sold themselves out to the lies of the day. Dominic felt himself a failure. Then Mary appeared with the Christ Child and taught Dominic how to pray her Rosary devotion – and the Dominicans would wear their long rosaries on their left side as weapons against evil from that apparition onwards! Eight hundred years later, no one sees me without first noticing the Rosary by which I am able to continually pray people to Christ through the hands of His Mother.

Even today, I love the night sky and when I gaze at the evening's moon, I now imagine Mother Mary calling me "daughter." In the spellbound grandeur of any starry night, I know I am safe – for all the world is held in the embrace of Mary's heavenly Rosary; her pledge of motherly protection for all who pray it. One by one, as the beads flow through our fingers, she lifts us up to her waiting Son! Oh, if only the entire world would know the Secret Power of the Rosary!

Editor's Note: To learn more about Sister Joseph Andrew's order – The Dominican Sisters of Mary, Mother of the Eucharist – check out page 91.

A BRIEF HISTORY *of* THE ROSARY

The Rosary is the most famous and most popular chaplet that we have as Catholics. A chaplet is a prayer devotion that commonly utilizes beads; it comes from a French word for "wreath" or "crown." While the structure and devotion of the Rosary has its roots with the "desert fathers," it is **St. Dominic** who is historically credited with giving the structured gift of the Rosary to the greater Church.

In the Rosary we meditate on the life of Christ, gazing upon Him through the lens and window of Mary's soul. Since she is our Blessed Mother, gifted to us from His Cross (**John 19:27**), it makes perfect sense that we would seek to look upon Christ in such an intimate and sinless way as she does. The Rosary draws us into more perfect discipleship and focuses our prayer on the Trinity.

The Rosary is a prayer on a group of beads that was developed as a way to teach the life of Christ and Mary to those who were not able to read. It was also developed to assist those who were not clergy in praying the Liturgy of the Hours, the prayer of the Church. In the prayer we take our intentions to Mary and show our honor and respect for her as the greatest of all the saints and an example to us all.

HOW TO PRAY THE ROSARY

The Rosary is divided into four sets of Mysteries: Joyful, Luminous, Sorrowful, and Glorious. It is intended as we pray each "Mystery" that we meditate on the meaning of the event in the life of Christ and Mary and also on the event in our own lives.
Each Mystery has five decades, and each decade corresponds to an event in the life of Christ. There are three basic prayers that are prayed: the Our Father, the Hail Mary, and the Glory Be. There is an optional prayer that some like to include in the Rosary called the Fatima prayer. At the end and the beginning of the Rosary there are a couple additional prayers such as the Apostles' Creed and the Hail Holy Queen.

THE MYSTERIES OF THE ROSARY

Joyful Mysteries (Mondays & Saturdays)

1. The Annunciation
2. The Visitation
3. The Nativity of Jesus
4. The Presentation of Jesus
5. The Finding of Jesus in the Temple

Luminous Mysteries (Thursdays)

1. The Baptism of Jesus
2. The Wedding at Cana
3. The Proclamation of the Kingdom
4. The Transfiguration
5. The Institution of the Eucharist

Sorrowful Mysteries (Tuesdays & Fridays)
1. The Agony in the Garden
2. The Scourging at the Pillar
3. The Crowning with Thorns
4. The Carrying of the Cross
5. The Crucifixion

Glorious Mysteries (Wednesdays & Sundays)
1. The Resurrection
2. The Ascension of Jesus
3. The Descent of the Holy Spirit
4. The Assumption of Mary
5. The Coronation of Mary

PRAYERS YOU'LL NEED TO KNOW

Apostles' Creed

I believe in God, the Father Almighty, Creator of heaven and earth and in Jesus Christ, His only Son, our Lord; Who was conceived by the Holy Spirit, born of the Virgin Mary, suffered under Pontius Pilate, was crucified, died, and was buried, He descended into hell; on the third day He rose again from the dead; He ascended into heaven, and is seated at the right hand of God, the Father Almighty; from there He will come to judge the living and the dead. I believe in the Holy Spirit, the holy catholic Church, the communion of saints, the forgiveness of sins, the resurrection of the body, and life everlasting. Amen.

The Lord's Prayer (Our Father)

Our Father, Who art in heaven, hallowed be Thy name; Thy Kingdom come, Thy will be done on earth as it is in heaven. Give us this day our daily bread; and forgive us our trespasses as we forgive those who trespass against us; and lead us not into temptation, but deliver us from evil. Amen.

Hail Mary
Hail Mary, full of grace, the Lord is with thee. Blessed art thou amongst women and blessed is the fruit of thy womb, Jesus. Holy Mary, Mother of God, pray for us sinners now and at the hour of our death. Amen.

The Doxology (Glory Be)
All Glory be to the Father, and to the Son, and to the Holy Spirit. As it was in the beginning, is now and ever shall be, world without end. Amen.

Fatima Prayer
O my Jesus, forgive us our sins. Save us from the fires of hell, and lead all souls to heaven, especially those in most need of Thy mercy. Amen.

Salve Regina (Hail Holy Queen)
Hail Holy Queen, Mother of Mercy, our life our sweetness and our hope. To thee do we cry, poor banished children of Eve; To thee do we send up our sighs, mourning and weeping in this valley of tears. Turn then, most gracious advocate, thine eyes of mercy toward us and after this our exile show unto us the blessed fruit of thy womb, Jesus. O clement, O loving, O sweet Virgin Mary! Pray for us O Holy Mother of God, that we may be made worthy of the promises of Christ. Amen.

ORDER TO SAY THEM IN

1. While holding the crucifix make the Sign of the Cross and then recite the **Apostles' Creed**.

2. Recite the **Our Father** on the first large bead.

3. Recite the **Hail Mary** for an increase of faith, hope, and love on each of the three small beads.

4. After the three **Hail Marys** recite the **Glory Be** and ***Fatima Prayer.**

5. Recall the first Rosary Mystery and recite the **Our Father** on the large bead.

6. On each of the adjacent ten small beads (referred to as the decade) recite a **Hail Mary** while reflecting on the mystery.

7. After the ten **Hail Marys** say the **Glory Be**, and the *__Fatima Prayer__ (O My Jesus).

8. Each succeeding decade is prayed in a similar manner by recalling the appropriate mystery, reciting the **Our Father**, ten **Hail Marys**, the **Glory Be**, and the *__Fatima Prayer__ while reflecting on the mystery.

9. When the fifth mystery is completed, the Rosary is customarily concluded with the **Hail Holy Queen**.

*optional

TAKING IT FURTHER

DIFFERENT WAYS TO PRAY THE ROSARY

In the following pages we will take a deeper look at all twenty mysteries of the Rosary. There are many ways that you can use the Rosary to reflect and pray. You can focus on the Scriptural passages that accompany the mysteries, or you can pray for growth in a specific virtue in each decade. The most beautiful part of praying a Rosary is that you can use the Rosary to reflect on different things each time you pray it.

In the next part of the book we wanted to help guide and focus your prayers within each mystery. If your mind tends to wander, hopefully these reflections will help keep you centered on the mystery at hand. If you don't struggle with focus, then perhaps these reflections will help you to go deeper into the mysteries and how they relate to your everyday life.

These reflections are in no way complete, they are a starting point intended to bless your prayer time. May the Lord bless you and shower you with grace as you meditate on His life through the Blessed Mother's eyes.

PRAYING THE ROSARY WITH SCRIPTURE

Take time to read the Scripture passages that accompany these mysteries. Ask the Lord to open your eyes and heart to see the ways in which He wants to speak to you through His Word. Ask Mary to accompany you on your journey through the Rosary.

JOYFUL MYSTERIES

The Annunciation - Luke 1:26-33, 38

The Visitation - Luke 1:39-45

The Nativity of Jesus - Luke 2:6-12

The Presentation of Jesus - Luke 2:25-32

The Finding of Jesus in the temple - Luke 2:41-50

LUMINOUS MYSTERIES

The Baptism of Jesus - Matthew 3:13-17

The Wedding at Cana - John 2:1-11

The Proclamation of the Kingdom - Mark 1:14-15

The Transfiguration - Matthew 17:1-8

The Institution of the Eucharist - Matthew 26:26-28

SORROWFUL MYSTERIES

The Agony in the Garden - Luke 22:39-46

The Scourging at the Pillar - Mark 15:6-15

The Crowning with Thorns - John 19:1-6

The Carrying of the Cross - John 19:16-22

The Crucifixion - John 19:25-30

GLORIOUS MYSTERIES

The Resurrection - Mark 16:1-7

The Ascension of Jesus - Luke 24:45-53

The Descent of the Holy Spirit - Acts 2:1-8

The Assumption of Mary - Luke 1:46-55

The Coronation of Mary - Revelation 12:1-17

ONE MINUTE REFLECTIONS

These quick one-line reflections are meant to help direct your Rosary. With each Hail Mary you pray in a decade, a one-line reflection is provided to help guide you during your prayer.

THE JOYFUL MYSTERIES

THE ANNUNCIATION

Our Father...

1. Hail Mary...
God sees more in you than you see in yourself.

2. Hail Mary...
How is God calling *you* to make Jesus present this day?

3. Hail Mary...
God desires to bless and use you, even in your youth.

4. Hail Mary...
Do you sometimes allow fear of the unknown affect your response to God's call?

5. Hail Mary...
God has a plan for your life that might not be consistent with your plans.

6. Hail Mary...
God's ways are not our ways.

7. Hail Mary...
What virtue or characteristic do you see in Mary that is most difficult for you to imitate?

8. Hail Mary...
Do you believe that God will bring to fulfillment what He promises?

9. Hail Mary...
Being faithful to God's plan can be difficult at times.

10. Hail Mary...
Would you have said "yes" if you were Mary or Joseph?

Glory Be...

THE VISITATION

Our Father…

1. Hail Mary…
Elizabeth greeted Mary joyfully. Do you share in others' joys?

2. Hail Mary…
The Holy Spirit was upon John, even in the womb.

3. Hail Mary…
In the presence of Jesus, John leaped in Elizabeth's womb. How are you moved in the presence of Jesus in the Eucharist?

4. Hail Mary…
Mary gave thanks and glory to God, even though she did not fully understand His plan.

5. Hail Mary…
What does it mean (to you) to "magnify the Lord"?

6. Hail Mary…
Are you magnifying Jesus by the way you live your daily life?

7. Hail Mary…
John proclaimed the presence of Jesus without using words.

8. Hail Mary…
How do your actions proclaim Jesus?

9. Hail Mary…
Mary went and served Elizabeth.

10. Hail Mary…
Is God calling you to service in some way?

Glory Be…

Our Father...

1. Hail Mary...
Mary said yes not only to one event, but she said yes to a journey.

2. Hail Mary...
What went through Joseph's mind when he held Jesus for the first time?

3. Hail Mary...
What does God's humble birth teach us about Him?

4. Hail Mary...
Did God supply a space when people wouldn't?

5. Hail Mary...
Why were shepherds invited first and not nobler local men?

6. Hail Mary...
Would you have followed the star?

7. Hail Mary...
Jesus depended on Mary for food, warmth, and care.

8. Hail Mary...
Mary is the Mother of God.

9. Hail Mary...
Joseph and Mary trusted God. Do you?

10. Hail Mary...
The King was laid upon a bed of straw, not a bed of silk. Do you ever let worldly comfort or materials affect your outlook on what is most important?

Glory Be...

THE PRESENTATION OF JESUS

Our Father...

1. Hail Mary...
Mary and Joseph offered their only son back to God, for His glory.

2. Hail Mary...
Do you give thanks to God for the things He gives you?

3. Hail Mary...
How did Simeon know that Jesus was the Messiah?

4. Hail Mary...
Have you been waiting for and looking for Jesus in your own life?

5. Hail Mary...
God speaks to us constantly.

6. Hail Mary...
How often do you stop and listen to God?

7. Hail Mary...
How did it make Mary feel to hear prophecies that spoke of her Son's suffering or death?

8. Hail Mary...
If it was your child, what would you do if others spoke out against Him?

9. Hail Mary...
We own nothing; all good gifts come from God.

10. Hail Mary...
Do you offer your gifts and blessings back to God or try to possess what is His?

Glory Be...

THE FINDING OF JESUS IN THE TEMPLE

Our Father...

1. Hail Mary...
Why did Jesus feel the need to head back to the Temple?

2. Hail Mary...
How often do you just listen to God?

3. Hail Mary...
Would you have left your family to go spend time at church?

4. Hail Mary...
Mary and Joseph only assumed that Jesus was with them. How many times in our lives do we assume things when God has other plans?

5. Hail Mary...
Did Jesus speak first or listen first?

6. Hail Mary...
Do you ever feel like people don't expect much of you, because of your young age?

7. Hail Mary...
How often do you stop worrying about the world and follow God's plan for you?

8. Hail Mary...
If you are to be like Jesus, you must be obedient to your parents.

9. Hail Mary...
How often do you trust your parents' guidance?

10. Hail Mary...
God reveals His plan(s) for you in His time, not yours.

Glory Be...

THE LUMINOUS MYSTERIES

BAPTISM OF THE JESUS

Our Father...

1. Hail Mary...
Do you believe that the Holy Spirit is with you?

2. Hail Mary...
What gifts do you desire most from the Holy Spirit?

3. Hail Mary...
You are God's beloved.

4. Hail Mary...
The ministry of Jesus was not private; He came for you.

5. Hail Mary...
What ministry has God designed you for?

6. Hail Mary...
Do you view the Holy Spirit as a person or as a dove?

7. Hail Mary...
John the Baptist's life pointed to Jesus. Does yours do the same?

8. Hail Mary...
How is God calling you to point your family to the Lord?

9. Hail Mary...
Baptism reveals God's desire for you to be part of His family.

10. Hail Mary...
Say a prayer for your godparents.

Glory Be...

THE WEDDING AT CANA

Our Father...

1. Hail Mary...
The disciples joined Mary and Jesus at the wedding feast.

2. Hail Mary...
You are invited to Jesus' wedding feast: the Mass.

3. Hail Mary...
Mary reminds us, "Do whatever He tells you."

4. Hail Mary...
Do you listen to what God is calling you to do?

5. Hail Mary...
Jesus turns the water into wine. Do you believe that God will work miracles in your own life?

6. Hail Mary...
What miracles do you need in your life?

7. Hail Mary...
Do your desires seek out God's will or your own?

8. Hail Mary...
Jesus produces an abundance of wine. He wants to shower His gifts upon you in abundance.

9. Hail Mary...
Jesus honors the request of His Mother. Do you invite Mary to pray with you?

10. Hail Mary...
Mary brought the situation to Jesus' attention and trusted in how He would act.

Glory Be...

THE PROCLAMATION OF THE KINGDOM

Our Father...

1. Hail Mary...
When Christ came, the Kingdom came with Him.

2. Hail Mary...
"The Kingdom of God is at hand. Repent and believe in the Gospel" (Mark 1:15).

3. Hail Mary...
Repent means to turn away from sin and to turn to God.

4. Hail Mary...
What do you need to repent of?

5. Hail Mary...
How are you going to avoid those sins in the future?

6. Hail Mary...
How can you turn even more to God?

7. Hail Mary...
Do you believe in the Gospel, really believe in it?

8. Hail Mary...
Jesus' Kingdom is not of this world. Do you desire things of this world or His Kingdom?

9. Hail Mary...
What worldly desires or goals do you need to let go of to grab hold of God?

10. Hail Mary...
Do you trust in God's will for your life, completely?

Glory Be...

THE TRANSFIGURATION

Our Father...

1. Hail Mary...
Jesus took His disciples to pray. Prayer is essential to following Christ.

2. Hail Mary...
When do you "get away" from the daily grind and go to pray with Jesus?

3. Hail Mary...
During prayer they had a powerful experience of God.

4. Hail Mary...
Moses and Elijah risked their lives to follow God and share His message.

5. Hail Mary...
Picture the scene of the Transfiguration. What does it look like in your imagination?

6. Hail Mary...
Where do you see God's glory in the Church?

7. Hail Mary...
Do you see God's glory in your everyday life?

8. Hail Mary...
"This is my chosen Son, listen to Him" (Luke 9:35).

9. Hail Mary...
What needs to change so you can listen more closely to God?

10. Hail Mary...
When you focus on the face of Jesus, do you look away or stare more deeply?

Glory Be...

INSTITUTION OF THE EUCHARIST

Our Father...

1. Hail Mary...
The command was, "Take and eat" not "take and understand" (C.S. Lewis).

2. Hail Mary...
At the Last Supper, Jesus celebrated the first Mass.

3. Hail Mary...
Do you *fully* participate in Mass every Sunday?

4. Hail Mary...
Do you remember the readings from last Sunday?

5. Hail Mary...
Do you sit as close, listen as closely, or sing as gratefully as you ought?

6. Hail Mary...
Jesus sacrificed Himself for us, how do you sacrifice yourself for Him?

7. Hail Mary...
Eucharist literally means "thanksgiving."

8. Hail Mary...
Jesus gave thanks; what do you have to be thankful for in your life?

9. Hail Mary...
Do you spend adoration time alone with Jesus before the Blessed Sacrament?

10. Hail Mary...
Say a prayer for your parish priests in thanksgiving for their vocation to the priesthood.

Glory Be...

THE SORROWFUL MYSTERIES

THE AGONY IN THE GARDEN

Our Father...

1. Hail Mary...
What distractions fill your mind as you prepare to pray this Rosary?

2. Hail Mary...
"My soul is sorrowful..." (Mark 14:34).

3. Hail Mary...
Share with your Father, like Christ, the cup (situation) you wish could be removed from your life at this time.

4. Hail Mary...
God desires that you trust in His will, and not your own.

5. Hail Mary...
Seek to live in Christ's light.

6. Hail Mary...
Pray that you can forgive someone who abandoned you in your hour of need.

7. Hail Mary...
Find the strength to forgive someone who has betrayed you.

8. Hail Mary...
Pray for souls who do not know God's love or mercy.

9. Hail Mary...
Pray for grace in times of temptation.

10. Hail Mary...
May the example of our Mother Mary instill in us the gift of perseverance and patience in seeking the will of God.

Glory Be...

THE SCOURGING AT THE PILLAR

Our Father...

1. Hail Mary...
Lord, forgive me for all the times I have torn people down with my words or actions.

2. Hail Mary...
"For he (Pontius Pilate) knew it was out of envy that the chief priests handed Him over" (Mark 15:10). Lord, reveal to me the people of whom I am envious?

3. Hail Mary...
Pray for God's forgiveness for both the things we do and fail to do.

4. Hail Mary...
When have you failed to speak for the truth or defend Christ?

5. Hail Mary...
The Lord calls you to be a voice for those with no voice.

6. Hail Mary...
When have you persecuted Christ in another?

7. Hail Mary...
God calls you to stand strong in times of difficulties and persecution.

8. Hail Mary...
Jesus suffered for the sins of all, including your sins.

9. Hail Mary...
God allowed Himself to suffer.

10. Hail Mary...
Suffering reveals true love.

Glory Be...

THE CROWNING WITH THORNS

Our Father...

1. Hail Mary...
Lord, reveal to me all the ways I live for the world and not for You.

2. Hail Mary...
When have you pierced another with mockery, sarcasm, or hurtful words?

3. Hail Mary...
Pray for forgiveness and healing for the times you have used hurtful words or committed hurtful actions.

4. Hail Mary...
Christ the King's crown wasn't made of earthly gold, but thorns.

5. Hail Mary...
Living for the Kingdom of heaven will get you persecuted on earth.

6. Hail Mary...
God alone is to be glorified and praised!

7. Hail Mary...
Who in your life lives boldly for Christ, regardless of mockery? Pray for them.

8. Hail Mary...
Lord, humble and purify me of all things that I have placed before You.

9. Hail Mary...
Lord, open my eyes to the people I mock and insult daily.

10. Hail Mary...
Lord, allow me to find it in my heart to love those who mock and insult me.

Glory Be...

THE CARRYING OF THE CROSS

Our Father...

1. Hail Mary...
The Lord is calling you to follow His example, to be strong in the darkness.

2. Hail Mary...
Do you trust that He has not abandoned you?

3. Hail Mary...
Give me the courage, Lord, to accept the cross I am called to carry.

4. Hail Mary...
God loves Jesus perfectly, and still allowed Jesus to suffer.

5. Hail Mary...
God loves you perfectly. If you suffer, it doesn't mean God has forgotten about you.

6. Hail Mary...
The Lord sends you people, like Simon, to help carry your crosses.

7. Hail Mary...
Who are you helping to carry their cross?

8. Hail Mary...
Like the weeping women, give me the courage to follow You when the crowd is jeering and cursing Your holy name.

9. Hail Mary...
Lord, when I fall, give me the strength to keep walking and to keep seeking you.

10. Hail Mary...
What are the burdens or "crosses" that come from your own sin that Christ wants to remove?

Glory Be...

THE CRUCIFIXION

Our Father...

1. Hail Mary...
"Father, forgive them for they know not what they do" (Luke 23:34). Lord, allow me to forgive others when they seek to hurt me.

2. Hail Mary...
Jesus chose the cross. Nails didn't hold Jesus down, they held Him up.

3. Hail Mary...
The salvation Jesus offers from the cross will take away all pain and suffering.

4. Hail Mary...
"Jesus, remember me when You come into Your kingdom" (Mark 23:42).

5. Hail Mary...
Jesus, be my Savior, today and forever!

6. Hail Mary...
Jesus said, "I thirst" (John 19:28). May I thirst for You alone, Lord Jesus.

7. Hail Mary...
Like Mary and the disciples who followed to Calvary, may we continually keep our eye on Christ in the midst of an evil generation.

8. Hail Mary...
Have you placed Christ on the cross this day?

9. Hail Mary...
Are you the thief asking merely for intervention or for total salvation?

10. Hail Mary...
"Today, you will be with Me in paradise" (Mark 23:43). Jesus wants you in heaven.

Glory Be...

THE GLORIOUS MYSTERIES

THE RESURRECTION

Our Father...

1. Hail Mary...
If Jesus didn't rise from the dead, you are not saved from death.

2. Hail Mary...
In what areas of your life do you feel dead or "entombed"?

3. Hail Mary...
Invite God to resurrect those "dead areas" of your life.

4. Hail Mary...
How did Mary feel on Good Friday?

5. Hail Mary...
Do you struggle to trust God when you are suffering?

6. Hail Mary...
What was Mary thinking on Easter morning?

7. Hail Mary...
Are you ever surprised by God's goodness?

8. Hail Mary...
Do the people in your world believe that Jesus is God?

9. Hail Mary...
Do your moral choices demonstrate someone who believes Jesus is alive?

10. Hail Mary...
Do you run out into the day passionately excited to tell people the "good news"?

Glory Be...

THE ASCENSION OF JESUS

Our Father...

1. Hail Mary...
Do you believe that Jesus is only "in heaven" or also on earth?

2. Hail Mary...
What did it look like when He ascended?

3. Hail Mary...
Heaven is not just for God, the angels, and saints. Heaven is for you.

4. Hail Mary...
Do you see heaven as your true home?

5. Hail Mary...
What needs to change in your life now to ensure heaven?

6. Hail Mary...
Your holy example will inspire others to live a holier life.

7. Hail Mary...
The apostles were nervous about "what to do next."

8. Hail Mary...
Didn't Jesus make His desires and our instructions clear enough before the Ascension? What does He want from you?

9. Hail Mary...
The angels told the disciples to quit standing there and get to work.

10. Hail Mary...
You have work to do for Jesus.

Glory Be...

THE DESCENT OF THE HOLY SPIRIT

Our Father...

1. Hail Mary...
God meets you where you are.

2. Hail Mary...
Are you open to where the Holy Spirit calls you to go?

3. Hail Mary...
The Holy Spirit destroys fear with boldness.

4. Hail Mary...
Are you open to speaking what the Spirit prompts you to say?

5. Hail Mary...
The Holy Spirit is power.

6. Hail Mary...
The Holy Spirit is within you.

7. Hail Mary...
Invite the Holy Spirit to breathe in you and through you.

8. Hail Mary...
Do you see clearly where the Holy Spirit is leading you?

9. Hail Mary...
Give me the courage to follow your way, Holy Spirit.

10. Hail Mary...
The Spirit is always before you and burning within you.

Glory Be...

THE ASSUMPTION OF MARY

Our Father...

1. Hail Mary...
Mary always is, was, and will be full of grace.

2. Hail Mary...
Mary didn't ascend into heaven, she was assumed.

3. Hail Mary...
Mary is unlike any other human who ever walked the face of the planet.

4. Hail Mary...
The love of Mary is truly glorious.

5. Hail Mary...
Mary's body never experienced corruption.

6. Hail Mary...
Mary is the perfect vessel of God.

7. Hail Mary...
How often to you reflect upon Mary's importance?

8. Hail Mary...
The grace of God overflowed from Mary.

9. Hail Mary...
Mary's a constant example and presence of faithfulness.

10. Hail Mary...
God honors Mary's sacrifice and surrender.

Glory Be...

THE CORONATION OF MARY

Our Father…

1. Hail Mary…
The Kingdom of heaven praised Mary in her perfection.

2. Hail Mary…
Mary's crown wasn't requested, only deserved.

3. Hail Mary…
Even as a Queen, humility still fills Mary's being.

4. Hail Mary…
Picture Mary, your Mother, enthroned in heaven.

5. Hail Mary…
Doesn't God honor Mary's requests?

6. Hail Mary…
Mary was set apart on earth as she is in heaven.

7. Hail Mary…
Christ welcomed Mary as Mother *and* Queen.

8. Hail Mary…
The Holy family on earth is the Royal family of heaven.

9. Hail Mary…
Honor Mary the way Christ honored her.

10. Hail Mary…
A lifetime of humble sacrifice is met with eternal glory and celebration.

Glory Be…

GOING EVEN DEEPER

These reflections are meant to take you deeper in prayer while praying the Rosary. We'll walk you through a brief reflection to put you into what is going on in the mystery. Then, read and reflect on how God is speaking to you through the events that surround the life of Christ. Let Mary walk with you and ask the Holy Spirit to open your heart to recognize Him moving in your life.

JOYFUL MYSTERIES - REFLECTIONS

1. THE ANNUNCIATION

Mary sat down with a thud on the hard, stone bench. "Be not afraid?" The light and power emanating from the messenger before her made her quake and tremble with fear. "Favored one?" She was a small and seemingly insignificant peasant girl from a nowhere town in a nowhere desert. And yet, even as confusion crossed her mind, her heart protested; she knew that she wanted God's will above anything else.

The prayers spoken in the silence of her heart, prayers offered at mealtime with her family, the prayers reflected in the Psalms that she heard at temple – they had all focused on the same thing: Make me your servant. She began to tremble again as the angel's power and presence revealed to her the form of service God was asking of her.

Fear is a normal and natural response to the wonder and awe of God's presence. Even Mary struggled with both confusion and fear when faced with the power and brilliance of God's heavenly messenger. But then Gabriel says the words that break through to her heart: "Do not be afraid, Mary."

Even then, Mary does not blindly accept the angel

Gabriel's words. "How can this be?" she asks. This is not a one-way relationship – God is not forcing Himself upon her and demanding her cooperation. He allows her to ask questions.

In the midst of her questions, the angel does not comfort her by telling her, "Everything will be okay." He doesn't promise her a life without worry or suffering. He says, "the Holy Spirit will come upon you, and the power of the Most High will overshadow you" (Luke 1:35). God's promise is that He will be with her along the way, that God will give her the strength to bear what she has to bear and to do what she has to do.

Ultimately, Mary's fiat (meaning, "Let it be") is the "yes" that changes the course of human history. Mary's courage can be a model to us not because she acted without fear, but because she acted in spite of her fear.

What about you? The God of the Universe, the Master of Creation, has great things in store for you. He is asking you to do something great for Him. Ask Him to reveal to you His plan for you. Allow yourself to respond – even with fear and confusion – as Mary did.

Take comfort in the words the angel spoke to Mary, the same message that can be found repeated hundreds of times in Scripture: "Do not be afraid." Allow yourself to be reassured and encouraged. Continue the conversation with God, being open and

honest about your questions and doubts. How can this be? Listen for the same assurance God gave to Mary – assurance of His love for you and His promise to be with you and give you everything you need. He gently and patiently awaits your response.

2. THE VISITATION

The pain of isolation Elizabeth had experienced as a 'barren woman' had begun to melt away the day her husband had returned from temple unable to speak but with amazing news. That day, she had known that her prayers had been answered and that her aching womb would finally carry life. Still, she had not realized how deep that loneliness had penetrated her soul until she heard that her cousin Mary was arriving to visit her. The anticipation of finally having someone with whom to share joy, worry, and the celebration of the Lord's promises to her was a relief to the years of longing for a child. As she stood, gazing across the hills and searching the road for some sign of her cousin's arrival, Elizabeth's soul soared in hopeful anticipation and joy, not only for herself, but for her cousin as well: for the angel who had visited her husband had visited her as well and had told her of yet another miracle. And Elizabeth, who knew what it meant to be shunned and to fear for her life, prayed for her cousin and for the tiny Messiah she carried within her.

It is not easy to set aside anxiety and worry in order to celebrate the joy of the Good News. Fear of the future, broken relationships, struggles in school, worry about what others think of you... whatever your worries are, they are real, but don't let your worries stop you from being able to see God work in your life. Some days it seems impossible to overcome a culture that daily tries to convince us that the news of Jesus isn't good and that it's pointless, difficult, and uncomfortable – or that it isn't even really news at all.

The key to living the urgent joy of the Gospel lies in Elizabeth's greeting to her cousin: "Blessed are you who believed that what was spoken to you by the Lord would be fulfilled." Mary traveled in haste – with passion, urgency, and joy – despite the very real concerns and conflicts of her situation, because she believed that God would honor His promises to her.

Do you believe that these promises that the Lord has spoken to you will be fulfilled?

Faith will transform you! The urgency of joy that radiates from you will begin to impact those around you. After all, the joy of Mary's faith was so contagious that John the Baptist, the prophet – still in Elizabeth's womb – was caught up in it and began celebrating.

3. THE NATIVITY OF JESUS

All of Bethlehem was dark and quiet when the Savior made His entrance into the world, and His first home was a small stable, surrounded by animals, their food, and their waste. But the physical poverty means nothing to the Infant in the protective circle of Mary's arms. It means nothing to Mary whose heart shines with both the tender, protective love of a mother holding her baby in her arms and the profound adoration of a soul adoring God in the flesh.

When you think of that holy night, how do you see it? Do you tend to idealize it—to imagine it as neat and tidy as the Nativity scenes found in your parish on Christmas Eve? Do you imagine the smells and sounds of the stable and think of the physical poverty that Jesus, Mary, and Joseph endured?

The physical poverty of the experience (no room in the inn, a smelly stable, lying the infant in the manger) is an outward sign of the inward state of Mary and Joseph's hearts. The poverty in their hearts is not physical, but the humble "poverty of spirit" that allows them to think first of God and not of themselves. This poverty of spirit leads them to trust that God will provide for them, as He has promised, even when things aren't going so well.

Jesus is born into the humble and dirty stable that night. The loving power of His presence makes the physical surroundings unnoticeable and immaterial. On this night, heaven and earth have met in a stable, but also in the souls of the Holy Family.

What about your heart? Jesus is born there as well – He was born there on that first Christmas, He is born there at your Baptism and He is born again there each time you receive the Sacraments. Is your heart neat and tidy and ready for the presence of the Savior? Or is it smelly, dirty, and a little run down?

He does not desire to be born into a place of perfect cleanliness and perfection; He perfects the place into which He is born. Allow the birth of Christ into your heart to change you, as it changed Mary and Joseph that night. Ask for the poverty of spirit to think first of God and not yourself.

4. THE PRESENTATION OF JESUS

Simeon's back ached from the long walk from his home to the temple. Little did he know what this day would hold for him. His body may have been slowing in his old age, but his soul had never felt more alive. The Spirit of the Lord had shown him a clearer vision than his aging eyes had seen in years. Before death claimed his body, he knew he would see the Christ, the Messiah, the Promised One of Israel.

A sound captured his attention, and he looked up. There, at the entrance gate, a father was attempting to wrangle his newborn child and the doves he had brought as sacrifice. Simeon glanced over to the purification gate and saw the new mother, fresh from the ritual bath, rush over to soothe the child as the father completed the ritual offering for his firstborn son. As soon as the doves had been offered, Simeon noticed with astonishment that he could see the family clearly though they were across the temple from him. Back aching no longer, he practically leaped up and ran to the young family – surely this was it! This was the moment the Lord had promised him!

In that moment, the aged Simeon, a holy man of God, recognizes and then proclaims, for the first time in public, the exalted identity and saving mission of Jesus Christ.

Do you always recognize Christ?

Simeon's elderly and possibly clouded eyes were able to recognize Jesus for who He was – his Savior. What is clouding your vision and preventing you from seeing Jesus as your Savior? Just as He did for Simeon, God will open your eyes to the powerful understanding of His mercy – that Jesus came in the flesh to offer Himself as a sacrifice for sin. Jesus Himself promises that He will speak to you – His voice is the voice of the Good Shepherd who calls you by name.

Do you recognize Him?

If you are having trouble seeing Jesus' power and grace working in your life, head to the Sacraments – especially the Eucharist. When you have trouble recognizing Jesus offering you guidance, direction, or purpose, read and meditate on the Scriptures. We do not need Jesus to be physically in our midst as He was to Simeon that day in order to see Him.

Do you recognize Him?

By His voice, in His Word, through the bread and cup, and by the miracles you will see Jesus clearly today. And when your eyes have been opened, then open your mouth! Proclaim, as Simeon did, through your words and your actions that Jesus has saved you and invite others to see Him as well.

5. THE FINDING OF JESUS IN THE TEMPLE

Her footsteps beat the prayer into the ground. It had been three days since they had last seen Jesus, and Mary was trying desperately not to give in to the panic that was clawing at her heart. They had searched high and low, but could not find Him. She remembered the fear of those first couple years after His birth, all those people who had tried to kill her son and the evil that sought to end His glorious mission. She prayed hard as she thought

back to the words of Simeon twelve years earlier, "A sword will pierce your heart" he had said. As she rounded the corner to the temple mount, she thought surely her heart would break out of fear and sorrow. Suddenly, in answer to her desperate pleas, she spotted Him at the foot of the stairs, listening and asking questions to the teacher.

Imagine the warring emotions and desires in Mary's heart in that instant. The desire to discipline her young son; relief and the desire to hold Him close; fear and the desire to never let Him out of her sight again. Scripture tells us that when He is finally found and questioned, His response startles them: ""Why were you looking for me? Did you not know that I must be in my Father's house?" (Luke 2:39).

Jesus understands that His identity as God's Son, and His obedience to His heavenly Father's will, take precedence over everything else. Mary and Joseph, however, "did not understand what He said to them" (Luke 2:50).

How many times have you felt that way about your parents? That they just do not understand you? Aside from giving His parents panic attacks, Jesus didn't do anything technically wrong. He was right to be about His Father's work. He was right that His identity as the Son of God took precedence over His earthly family. It can be frustrating when parents, or others in authority, keep you from being who it is you want to be or from doing the things you want to do.

Jesus, however, does not let frustration or His desire to be "right" take over. Instead of fighting, arguing, or trying to convince His parents that He was right and they were wrong, Scripture tells us that Jesus "went down with them and came to Nazareth, and was obedient to them" (Luke 2:51).

Jesus' obedience to His parents, even when they were "wrong" is an example you can turn to when you are justifiably frustrated or angry with your own parents – or anyone else in authority. Ask Jesus to help you desire the same listening posture and prayerful obedience to authority that He demonstrated – especially when you are frustrated or know you are right.

LUMINOUS MYSTERIES - REFLECTIONS

1. THE BAPTISM OF JESUS

His eyes surveyed the scene. The crowd gathered on the shore of the mighty River Jordan, entering one by one to be renewed and "made clean" by the wild and prophetic Baptizer named John. As Jesus drew near the water, He did the unthinkable...God, Himself, asked to be baptized. The sinless One offered a humble and holy example, one that calls us all to follow in His sacred footsteps. As the water fell from Christ's brow, the sky "ripped open" and the Spirit descended. The Father's voice boomed from heaven leaving no doubt of His love for His child(ren) when He said, "This is my beloved Son; with thee I am well pleased" (Mark 1:9-12). Those privileged to witness such a sight were no doubt left speechless during it and anything following it. But why Baptism? Why water? In the days of Noah and of Moses we saw the power of God bring death and new life through water. It was Joshua who, in this same historic river, would lead God's children into the Promised Land centuries before Jesus saw His saintly cousin. There, in that luminous moment, the Trinity was present once again to lead God's children to freedom - a freedom from sin and despair into a life of peace and blessing.

Do you ever wonder if God loves you - I mean really loves you? Do you ever fall into that trap of thinking that God's love for you varies based upon how you act?

Don't. Don't fall into that trap.

Read that line from the Gospel again, "You are my beloved son; with thee I am well pleased." God wasn't just talking to Jesus...He is talking to you. Whether a man or woman, through the grace of your Baptism you have been claimed and named - you are a son or a daughter of God. Is that too hard to believe, too incredible to grasp? Good, then the next decade is a great place to start. Feel the humid air next to the river Jordan while you pray. Listen to the running water. See the dove fall and hear the voice of your heavenly Father reminding you that His love is not conditional, it is perfect. Nothing you do can make God love you more and nothing you do can make God love you less. Our sin affects our ability to receive His love but doesn't do anything to lessen His love for us. And the next time you dip your hands in that holy water and make the sign of the cross, remember your Baptism, the gift you were given, the water of the Jordan that preceded it and that the Trinity who was present then is still present to you.

2. THE WEDDING AT CANA

The celebration must have been immense. To run out of wine only three days into the feast? These celebrations usually spanned a week! People had traveled dozens of miles, many on foot, to pray and to witness a marriage. And now the Blessed Virgin scans the crowd to find her Son. Hoping to spare the couple any embarrassment, the Mother seeks a carpenter to help the wedding waiters. She approaches Jesus humbly and with a simple statement. "They have no wine." She doesn't specifically ask her Son to act. The Mother doesn't "tell" Him what to do. She merely brings a situation to His divine attention and trusts that God's will shall be done.

Jesus' true identity, however, was not yet public; even the small gathering who had witnessed His miraculous Baptism and the handful that had decided to follow Him were still coming to understand Who exactly it was that stood in their midst. Why here? Why now? Why would this marriage reception be the setting for Christ to perform His first miracle and by doing so, reveal His identity with such a sign?

It was in this moment, that the God who commanded us to "honor thy father and mother" would show us just how serious He is and just how important our mother Mary will forever be. At her request, the Lord changed average water into the finest wine any in Cana had tasted. The celebration continued not because of the love between Cana's bride and groom, but because of the love of a Son for His Mother and the love of that Son (the groom) for His bride, the Church.

Do you ever feel like your prayer requests are unimportant or that your life is somehow insignificant? You aren't the first but you also couldn't be further from the truth. No prayer request, no hope or dream, no concern or anxiety is insignificant to God. If it matters to you, it matters to the One Who created you. Now, that doesn't mean that you'll get everything that you pray for (that wouldn't be good for us), nor does it mean that everything we stress about is worthy of stress. What it means is that when we go to God, He promises us that He listens to us (just check out Jeremiah 29:12).

Mary gives us a really important example of humility and of trust at Cana. Mary wasn't trying to manipulate Jesus' power before it was time. This wasn't about trying to "change Jesus' mind" about how or when to demonstrate His divinity. Mary and Jesus share the same blood and the same heart for their heavenly Father. Mary's petition to Jesus was a prayer of humility. She brought a situation that troubled her to Jesus' attention, and then she just trusted in whatever God's will was and that it would happen through Jesus' intercession. If Jesus had declined, it would not have meant that Mary was unloved. The fact that

Jesus honored Mary's request, though, shows us something about God's heart for her and about the honor she holds in heaven.

As Catholics, we are always encouraged to develop this type of relationship with our Blessed Mother, one in which we go to her, pray with her and ask her to pray for us (intercede) on our behalf to her Son. In honoring her, we obey the Commandments (the fourth to be specific) and we act as Jesus acted. Ask yourself, if we're called to be like Jesus, shouldn't that start with how we treat our parents (both earthly and heavenly)?

3. THE PROCLAMATION OF THE KINGDOM

The people had grown tired. Hope was in short supply. Hundreds of years had passed since the nation of Israel was a true Kingdom. The days of King David and King Solomon were distant memories, replaced by generations enslaved by foreign rulers. Mighty nations and kingdoms had overtaken Israel time and time again and now, the Roman Empire was ruling Israel on their own soil. God's children in Israel held onto hope...hope that God would one day fulfill His promise to give them a King forever, a King who would put the nations beneath His mighty feet. For generations they waited for the prophecies to be fulfilled, for their promised King to come in power and to exalt them above every other nation.

Enter the carpenter from a tiny town called Nazareth.

To say that Jesus "wasn't quite what people were expecting" would be a huge understatement. He didn't "look" like a King. He didn't walk like a King or consort with the types of people that royalty hung out with...but when He spoke, people listened. When Jesus acted, people took notice. When Christ preached, hearts were opened and souls were turned. And when Christ worked miracles, earth witnessed heaven right before them. The King of kings came not on a chariot but in a manger, and when His ministry began, the Lord left no doubt that He remembered His humble beginnings. He reached out to the oppressed, to the sinner, to the blind, the sick and the lame. In Christ's presence, the outcast was given VIP status and the egos of the proud were reduced to dust.

Put simply, when the King came, the Kingdom came with Him...and Jesus came to announce that it was a new day, that the time had come and the waiting was over. The time for the Kingdom of heaven was now and the King was establishing a headquarters for heaven on earth, His living Church. All were invited to join Him and to experience what a true Kingdom, with power rooted in love, actually looked like.

At Mass we often hear that "heaven and earth are filled with His glory."

Do you believe that? Is that what you think when you watch the news or scroll through your Twitter feed? Beyond shots of sunsets or amazing desserts, how often do you see the glory of God on your Instagram? Is earth really filled with God's glory because it can be pretty hard to see it.

Catholics are invited to see differently, though, and through these luminous mysteries, to be "enlightened" to see things from a broader perspective, to see things through Mary's eyes. Look at the line of sinners wanting to become saints outside the confessional. Look at brides and grooms still wanting to get married in an actual church before an altar of sacrifice, pledging their lives to one another. Look at men lying on their faces swearing their lives and obedience to the holy priesthood. Look at young women and men peacefully kneeling while making final vows in a religious order.

Consider every time you proudly wear that retreat t-shirt to school, lead a prayer before a game or a meal in public, witness to your love of God online or reach out to pray with and help a friend in need...in all those times, the Kingdom of God is being proclaimed.

Each and every time you live out your faith with humble boldness and unashamedly announce to the world that you are proud to be a Catholic, you - like Jesus - are proclaiming the Kingdom to the world, and with that proclamation, inviting them to come and experience the love of Christ in His Church.

4. THE TRANSFIGURATION

The other nine apostles grew smaller with each step up the path, as Jesus allowed only Peter, James and John to accompany Him atop the mountain. This wasn't the first time the Lord had taken only His "inner circle" of friends along separately but it would be the most memorable. What the three witnessed next didn't only change their day, it changed their lives. It was at that moment that the eyes of the apostles' minds and hearts were opened as they visually witnessed Jesus "transfigured."

All of a sudden, Jesus' clothes were a purity of white they'd never laid eyes on and His face shined so brightly that the sun paled in comparison. Before they knew it, the four of them weren't alone anymore - they were joined by heroes of the faith, Godly men through whom God had changed the world. The apostles actually saw Moses and Elijah talking with Jesus. The moment was so epic and the scene so captivating that Peter's only desire was to stay, wanting to put up tents and never leave, proclaiming, "It is good that we are here."

Jesus could have left all twelve at the bottom of the mountain. He could have gone off to pray alone like He had so many times before but He didn't. He chose the ones whose hearts were ready to receive what God wished to reveal to them. Their mortal eyes were allowed to witness the immortal. In that moment in time, they experienced the Timeless One in all of His glory.

Notice that it was only after a long walk up the high mountain that the Lord gave His closest followers a taste of what is to come for all of us, a foreshadowing of the beauty and peace and glory of God that awaits all of us who are willing to follow Him.

The mountain is important. Why not beside the sea like so many other teachings and miracles? Why not in the boat on the sea like the others?

When scaling a mountain, many things occur. Your perspective changes. Your effort changes. Steps aren't easy, they require effort. Breathing isn't easy, it requires more work. You feel every step, notice every hardship and have to keep pushing forward. It's a great metaphor for the Christian life... because when you keep following the Lord and keep pushing through the journey, you don't see things the same way. Those problems that seem huge at ground level really aren't so huge anymore, they're tiny. The closer you stay to the Lord and the higher you allow Him to take you and call you - the closer you are to heaven.

You have friends in your life or school or youth group who aren't yet walking with Jesus. You have others who are but who still want to remain in the world, feet planted in what is comfortable and popular. You'll have other friends who are following closer but not yet ready to fully surrender to Christ... they're camping at the bottom of the mountain. What about you? Are you living a bold life for Christ? Are you abandoned to all He wants for you and wants to give you? Is He calling you to scale the mountain behind Him? Because what He wants to reveal to you will only be seen once you've left everything else behind and you're following only Christ.

5. THE INSTITUTION OF THE EUCHARIST

There were drops of water scattered across the floorboards of the holy ground. The basin and the towel had been returned to their place. The apostles returned to their eating position, after having their feet washed clean by the God of the universe. This was no ordinary meal. How could it be after witnessing such an act of service and self-sacrifice on the part of the Lord? Nothing, though, could have prepared them for what happened next.

The bitter herbs were placed out. The unleavened bread was within reaching distance. The wine had been poured and the blessing(s) proclaimed. On the surface, it looked like the customary Passover supper; but looks can be very deceiving.

In the moments that followed, the words spoken and actions taken changed history and eternity, forever.

"This is my body."
"This is my blood."

The bread and wine were shared but they weren't mere grain or grapes anymore, their earthly form now veiled a heavenly substance. The apostles had been told previously that Jesus would give them His own flesh to eat, but they didn't fully comprehend it. They'd heard the Lord prophecy about how He would have to give His very life but they prayed it wasn't true. Now, just hours before Christ's body and blood would be taken on a cross, they were being given it at the table. He Who would soon be put to death was offering true and everlasting life. It was at this meal that everything changed.

You have no idea how highly God thinks of you. He created you, yes. He claimed you at your Baptism as His son or daughter, of course. He provides for you, blesses you, protects you, and sends people into your life to guide you, absolutely. But have you ever stopped to consider "why" He gave us the Eucharist?

The God of the universe thinks so highly of you that He allows Himself to literally dwell within you.

He didn't have to do it this way. He could have just decided to dwell in you spiritually and leave it at that. It didn't have to be so physical or so tangible. God could have opted not to give us the Eucharist, knowing that countless would take for granted what an amazing blessing it is, but He didn't. God loves us so much that He offers us - physical beings - His own physical presence and touch through the Sacraments.

It's easy to get caught up into the "hows" of the Eucharist. "How" does bread become flesh? "How" does the wine become His blood? "How" does this work with the priest? When we ask the "how" we miss the more important question of "why?"

Why would God choose to do this for us? Why does God humble Himself and make Himself so available in this way? Why would He use priests or do it through a common meal or command us to do it so often?

Maybe, just maybe God thinks more highly of us than we do of ourselves - and maybe God knows better what we really need than we do. When you receive the Eucharist, you're not consuming Him, He is consuming you with His love. God wants to change us from the inside out. When we receive God's body and blood, we receive His very life (called "grace") into our bodies and souls.

Just as it happened with the apostles in the upper room, this meal changes everything - and it's available to you at every single Mass.

SORROWFUL MYSTERIES - REFLECTIONS

1. THE AGONY IN THE GARDEN

The darkness of night swept through the garden but Jesus couldn't fall asleep knowing that His hour was quickly approaching. He knew the suffering that He was about go through and felt extreme sorrow for the sins of the entire world. He knew the betrayal and agony that was about to happen, a betrayal that brought with it death. He asked His friends to stay up and keep watch while He prayed, but they couldn't keep themselves away from sleep. Feeling alone, His knees fell to the floor and He spoke to the one He knew would never abandon Him: His Father. The cost of our sin was His very life. The weight of the world was before Him and His sweat turned to blood. He begged His Father to let this cup pass by Him, but He courageously said, "not what I will but what You will."

How often do you think about the suffering that Christ went through because of your sins? In the garden of Gethsemane centuries ago, Christ didn't just know about the betrayal that was about to happen with Judas, He felt the betrayal of each small sin ever committed. He knew that even though He was about to die for our sin, people would still hurt

Him, persecute His people, and doubt that He even existed.

Although the pain that our sin brought was great, nothing outweighed the mercy that was poured out for us on the cross. He knows your sins and wants to forgive you. He knows all things, even the things that you are most ashamed of and have hidden from Him. He wants to be reunited and reconciled with you. The pain that He felt in the garden was out of love for you. Have you gone to Him in the Sacrament of Reconciliation for forgiveness? Do you trust in His mercy?

His heart aches for yours. Bring Him into the darkest of places in your hearts. He will stay there and keep watch. He will never abandon you. He has always loved you and will never stop loving you. He embraced the suffering knowing that you might choose to love Him.

2. THE SCOURGING AT THE PILLAR

The crowds had gathered to see what the fate would be for Jesus. They hated and reviled Him, although just days before they were praising Him. They chose to set free a guilty criminal to convict a man whom was innocent. "Crucify Him!" the bloodthirsty mob shouted. Pilate gave the crowds their criminal, Barabbas, and handed Jesus over to be scourged.

The hands that had once healed were chained together, His arms wrapped around a stone pillar. His garments were moved over to expose His back. The soldiers gathered their instruments to inflict pain onto His body. The lashes tore into His skin, and no longer was His skin smooth and bare, but rather torn and bloodied. Maddened with fury, the soldiers continued to strike Him, until their own strength began to wear down.

Has there even been a moment in your life when you just feel like you cannot take one more thing going wrong? When things continue to pile up, it can be easy to feel alone and worn out. But the thing that we cannot forget is that when we suffer, we are not alone.

God, in His infinite love, suffered not only for us but with us. When we feel the need to complain about our current situations, never forget that Christ patiently endured His suffering and ultimately that suffering led to the greatest joy ever imagined: the Resurrection.

When you are in the face of great trials, ask God for the grace to endure the suffering virtuously. God will never give you more than you can handle. When you unite your suffering to Christ, His strength will be yours. Offer your suffering up to Christ and never forget how much He endured for you.

3. THE CROWNING WITH THORNS

His frail, broken body stood wearily in the courtyard. The soldiers that had just finished shredding apart His back, began to prod and push Him to begin to walk. The blood, beginning to dry, clung to the clothes that He wore. With each footstep He took, blood seeped onto the floor beneath Him and pain shot through His entire body.

The soldiers, looking for more ways to tear Him apart, began to mock and ridicule Him. They ripped the clothes off His broken back, exposing His wounds, and they threw a purple cloak over Him. They weaved a crown out of thorns and pressed it onto His head. The crown became one with Him, as each thorn cut through skin. Blood, sweat, and the soldier's spit dripped from His face and even though He suffered greatly, He continued on His path to Calvary.

Have you ever shirked away from making the Sign of the Cross in public, afraid that others will see you? Or have you ever felt that you are alone while defending the Church's stance on sexuality, marriage, or abortion? Mockery and persecution are never far from those who live out the Faith. But, when people attack you for your beliefs or morals or poke fun at the fact that you will not participate in sin, do not grow weary. The world criticizes the Faith because it directly contradicts what the world thinks is normal.

The suffering that Christ went through on His way to Calvary was both physical suffering and emotional suffering. He endured both. When the soldiers mocked Him, He did not lose heart or conviction. He knew what the cost of our sin would be. He felt the stings that mockery brought both in His physical body, but also in His heart. He understood the loneliness that can often accompany those that refuse to bow down to the standards of the world. We must never forget the promises that Christ made to us, "Blessed are those who are persecuted for the sake of righteousness, for theirs is the kingdom of heaven" (Matthew 5:10).

4. THE CARRYING OF THE CROSS

The crowds pressed themselves into the streets to witness the condemned man make His way up to Golgotha. What they unknowingly saw, however, was an innocent man embracing the fate of the guilty. His damaged body bore the weight of a splintered, wooden cross and His legs grew wearier with each step that He took. His fingers clung to the cross as His shoulders pushed forward. His death was looming around each corner and His exhaustion was evident with each fall that He took.

His brief interaction with His sorrowful mother gives Him some relief, but His strength is rapidly waning. The weight of the cross upon His frail, failing body is killing Him too quickly. The soldiers – out of fear of Him dying before they could crucify Him – pull a bystander from the crowds towards Jesus. Simon the Cyrenian has no choice but to help Jesus carry the cross. As the weight of the wood shifts from one shoulder to two, his eyes catch a glimpse of Jesus'. Simon comes face to face with Mercy and his heart burned with compassion for this man. Simon would never be the same after this encounter, and the two continued on the journey towards the crucifixion.

There are times when God sends us someone or something to lift us in our times of trouble. Whether it's a friend that calls us out of the blue to affirm us or a random gift that cheers us up on bad day, God is always reaching out to us in our times of need. God wants us to know that we are loved, and He gives us little reminders of that from time to time.

There are times, however, that we can miss out on those little expressions of God's compassion and love. We can be blind to the ways that God is trying to ease our burden when we let sin or pride cloud our vision. Instead of accepting a compliment, we dodge away from it. Instead of letting someone help us, we can think we can handle everything on our own. We can even fail to see when God might be gently encouraging us to reach out to someone else. That one girl in the class that no one talks to, how often do we sit next to her and see how she's doing? Or that guy who is always sarcastic and says hurtful things, do we fail to realize that his family is completely broken and he is in desperate need of a kind word?

Imagine what would have happened if Simon would have decided to not help Jesus in His time of need. He would have never come face to face with the Author of Life, with Jesus Himself. When we reach out to someone or we let someone help us, we can come face to face with Christ.

5. THE CRUCIFIXION

The journey to where He would be crucified was long and trying. The soldiers threw the cross from His shoulders onto the ground and Jesus fell with it. A soldier grabbed His right arm and another grabbed His left. Dragging his broken body onto the cross, they placed His right hand onto the wood. The thuds of the hammers hitting the nails temporarily silenced the crowd. Systematically they moved from one hand, to the next, and then to His feet.

As the soldiers began to position the cross into the ground to stand, the beloved disciple, Mary, and Mary of Magdala witnessed the horrific showcase of their friend's wounded body upon the splintered cross. With each breath He took, their sorrow was tangible. Jesus could have saved Himself from such a horrific death, but His love for humanity held

Him onto the cross. The nails that inflicted wounds into His hands and feet would be the means in which our healing was won. His breath became shallow and His strength began to fade, but His mercy and compassion did not. Forgiving even while dying on the cross, Christ took our place.

The sky grew dark and the earth began to quake. Silence swept the crowds as Jesus cried out loudly "'Father, into your hands I commend my spirit'; and when He had said this He breathed His last" (Luke 23:46).

The price had been paid. The veil was ripped. It is finished.

Jesus took on every sin ever committed: past, present, and future sin. He could have saved Himself from such a horrific death, but He chose to offer us salvation instead. He saved us. He paid our debt.

Satan thought that evil had been victorious, but the work of salvation was just beginning. His love is far more powerful than death itself.

Christ did not have to die for us. He chose to love us that much. Do we always choose to love God in all moments or do we turn our backs on Him? Do we recognize that the debt He paid was not just for those present two thousands years ago, but for us? God was willing to go as far as it took to offer you Salvation. But how far are you willing to go for Him?

Are you willing to face humiliation or persecution? Are you willing to go to Mass every Sunday and even daily? Will you go and "make disciples of all nations" (Matthew 28:10)? Will you pray daily? Will you avoid whatever leads you to sin and strive to be like Him?

The crucifix is a constant reminder to us of how far God was willing to go for us. Let our life be a constant witness to others of how far we are willing to go for Him.

GLORIOUS MYSTERIES - REFLECTIONS

1. THE RESURRECTION

Just as the sun began to peak above the horizon, the women set off to anoint the body of Jesus. How mournfully they walked as they remembered the events just two days before. As they slowly approached the tomb they asked each other, "Who will roll away the stone for us...?" (Matthew 16:3). Upon arriving and seeing that the stone was already rolled away, what were their thoughts? Did they feel betrayed, astonished, hopeful, or did they just feel nothing, numb from all the sorrow? As they stopped to enter the tomb, imagine their shock as they saw a man, not Jesus, dressed in white. Sensing their fear, he spoke these words, "Do not be amazed; you seek Jesus of Nazareth, who was crucified. He has RISEN!" (Mark 16:6).

With great fear and excitement, the women burst forth from the tomb and ran as fast as they could to tell the apostles what they had witnessed. When they reached the apostles, they began to tell of their encounter and before they could finish, Peter and John, darted off to see for themselves. Peter, gasping for air as he entered the tomb, saw the burial cloths neatly folded. Jesus was not there. Did Peter know how to reconcile the fear and joy he

must have felt in seeing this sight? Could it really be true that Jesus had risen from the dead?

Do I truly believe that Jesus has risen from the dead? Does that make any difference in my life? Do I believe that He has the power to burn away my sinfulness and fill me with His love?

Do I really believe that Jesus' Resurrection means that Satan no longer has a hold on my soul? Has it really hit me that Jesus died so that I could live eternally? Do I actually understand my total need for Him in my life? Do I realize that if Jesus hadn't died and rose from the dead that I would have no hope of salvation?

2. THE ASCENSION OF JESUS

After His Resurrection, Jesus spent forty days with His apostles, explaining the Scriptures and preparing them to be missionaries to the world. The time had come, however, for Jesus to mount the throne prepared for Him by the Father. How might the disciples have felt knowing that their teacher was no longer going to be with them? Had they learned enough to be effective evangelists? Did they question why Jesus had chosen them to be His witnesses to the ends of the earth? Did they feel worthy enough to be His servants? Jesus told them that He would send His Spirit and that He would empower them to do the work Jesus asked. But did they believe that His grace would be enough? Did the disciples feel hopeful, scared, or mystified at seeing Jesus ascend body and soul into heaven? How they must have yearned to be with Him at that moment and how much more would they desire to be with Him in the time that followed. Jesus' absence must have kindled a fire within their heart to tell the whole world about this God-man who had destroyed the power of the devil by the wood of a cross. Jesus would not and could not be forgotten.

There is a Latin phrase, "Momento Mori" which literally means, "Remember your death." While it may seem morbid and maybe scary to think of your death, we must always remember that this life is not all we are made for. There is another place, a more glorious place, that Jesus has prepared for us, if we remain faithful to Him. In this present time, it's easy to get caught up in many things that distract us from our end goal of heaven. What sort of things keep you from putting the Lord first in your life? Relationships? Phone? Texting? Busyness? Laziness? Lack of commitment to a prayer time? Do you truly believe in the life that is yet to come? What is one small commitment you can make today to "Momento Mori" (remember your death)?

3. THE DESCENT OF THE HOLY SPIRIT

On the day of Pentecost, all the disciples were gathered in one place. After witnessing the Ascension, imagine how inadequate the apostles must have felt... how would they be able to teach all people about Jesus? The task of evangelization that was set before them was daunting, even crippling. What about cultural and language barriers? Could they really do all that Jesus had commanded? Then, in the midst of all their fear and doubt, the Holy Spirit came in and sounded like "a rush of a mighty wind" and "tongues of fire" appeared upon their heads. If they had doubted Jesus' words before His Ascension, they surely didn't doubt it now. The Holy Spirit had come in His strength and power to burn away all insecurities and fear. Filled with God's own Spirit, the apostles flung wide open the doors and preached about the saving works of Jesus.

People were in town in Jerusalem from all over the world and every man could hear them speaking in their own native language! Did the passersby now understand what they had seen on Calvary? Could they sense the indescribable joy of the disciples? Was that enough to bring them to Jesus? Imagine the apostles' amazement when three thousand were converted by the power of the Holy Spirit... three thousand! How relieved must the apostles have felt when they realized they had only to be receptive to the Holy Spirit and He would do all the work. Had the apostles even come close to imagining how the Spirit would empower them?

Does the call to holiness seem too hard to attain, especially when you look at the sinfulness in your life? Do you depend on your own ability to be holy or do you depend on the Holy Spirit to lead and draw your heart to Jesus? Do you actually recognize your need for the Holy Spirit in your life?

The Holy Spirit speaks in the silence. How often do you spend time in silence, listening for Him to speak? Consider not listening to music when you normally do in the car or whenever you have down time. Train yourself to be taught in the silence... and work your way up! Start out with five minutes and when you can listen for five, add one more minute, with the sole task of listening to the Spirit. He desires to empower you with His Life! The same Holy Spirit that worked in the lives of the apostles desires to work in your life; you have only to invite Him.

4. THE ASSUMPTION OF MARY

The Assumption of Mary celebrates when Our Mother was taken up body and soul into heaven. Mary is the first believer in the Gospel and the first to experience the fruits of redemption. Where Mary goes, we hope to follow. Tradition holds that

Mary "fell asleep" and then peacefully passed from this world to the next. Death is usually a very difficult reality for us to face, but for someone who is without sin, this passing must have been surrounded with serenity and joyful anticipation. What do you think our Lady's last words on Earth were? How her heart must have burned with desire to be united once again with her Son. Her life was totally consecrated in love to Him. Mary did not travel to the ends of the Earth evangelizing, but she is the greatest saint. How is Mary the ultimate model of sanctity? What is it about this woman that God found so worthy to take her up, body and soul, into heaven? How beautiful is it that God allowed such perfection to be found in a lowly woman?

Our Lady is the perfect example of trust. From the time the Angel Gabriel asked if she would be the Mother of God all the way to her Assumption, she relied on the Lord to take care of the smallest details of her life. She didn't worry. She was confident in Jesus. She knew His plan was greater than the present circumstances. Do you truly believe that Jesus is concerned about the smallest details of your life? Do you believe that Jesus has a plan for your life? Do you actually believe that God has created you for something more beautiful than you can imagine? Do you truly believe that in loving Jesus and serving Him that you will receive all that your heart desires? Have you asked yourself what your heart truly desires? Do you have a relationship with your heavenly Mother?

How can you cultivate a relationship with the person who knew the heart of Jesus better than anyone else?

5. THE CORONATION OF MARY

After Mary was taken up into heaven, she was crowned Queen of heaven and Earth. She was given dominion over all creatures and she shares in the Eternal reign of Christ the King! Being Queen, she participates fully in Jesus' victory over sin and death. Her scepter of humility and crown of virtue makes Satan flee from her presence. Her obedience to her Son and her meekness is no match for the empty promises of the Tempter. She is strength; Satan is weakness. She is the moon who reflects the light of the Son. Her Coronation radiates God's divine mercy on the human race.

As sons and daughters of the King, we have been given authority over our sins, but too often we don't use that authority to conquer the areas in our life that lead us away from Jesus. We have control over our lives when we can freely say no to what harms us. Are there any areas in your life in which Satan sits enthroned? What can you do to abdicate his throne and bring the Victory of Christ to those areas?

Our Lady is a powerful intercessor because she was completely faithful to Jesus. Ask her to pray for you and be with you in your darkest hours.

FREQUENTLY ASKED QUESTIONS

ABOUT THE ROSARY

Is reciting the Our Father and Hail Mary the same as the "babbling" in prayer that Jesus warned us not do?

> *"And in praying, do not heap up empty phrases as the Gentiles do, for they think that they will be heard for their many words. Do not be like them, for your Father knows what you need before you ask him." – Matthew 6:7-8*

We've all heard people praying the Rosary. Sometimes it sounds like heart felt pleas and other times like a mindless drone. In cases of the latter, one has to question, "Did Jesus warn us against this? Is it wrong to pray repetitive prayers?" The answer lies in examining exactly how the pagans prayed. Pagans, during Jesus' time, would repeat the god's name over and over to get the attention of the god and thus have a higher chance of their prayer being answered. They did not have faith that their god paid any attention to them, so they made sure to act in a certain way or do a certain thing so their request would be fulfilled. Jesus warns against this calculated faith, "If I do this and this then God will surely answer me." How many times have we fallen into bargaining with God? Jesus wants us to approach the Father in trust knowing that He makes all things work together for our good (Romans 8:28). Jesus is not criticizing repetitive prayer; in fact He, as a faithful Jew, would recite the Scriptures daily. When we pray the Hail Mary or the

[1] Hahn, Scott, Curtis Mitch, and Dennis Walters. *The Gospel of Matthew: With Introduction, Commentary, and Notes and with Study Questions*. San Francisco: Ignatius. 2000. Print.

Our Father, we are praying the Scriptures and fulfilling St. Paul's command to "pray without ceasing" (1 Thessalonians 5:17).

Does the Rosary focus on Mary or on Jesus?

The Rosary is a meditation on the Word of God, who is Christ Himself. The phrases within the Hail Mary are straight from Scripture: "Hail Mary, full of grace, the Lord is with you" (Luke 1:28) and "Blessed are you among women and blessed is the fruit of your womb" (Luke 1:42). The words of the Hail Mary help us to focus in on the miracle of the Incarnation, the moment when the Eternal Son became flesh in the womb of a woman. Mysteries of the Rosary are a meditation on the life, death and Resurrection of Christ. The last two Mysteries of the Glorious Mysteries seem to focus on Mary, but in reality, it is a celebration of what God wants to offer us through His Son. Mary, the mother of God, experiences the first fruits of salvation. Where she goes, we hope to follow. When we reflect on her Assumption and Coronation we reflect on "what God has prepared for those who love Him" (1 Corinthians 2:9). We ask Mary to "pray for us sinners now and at the hour of our death" so that we too may celebrate the victory Christ has won for us, in this present time and in the life yet to come.

What is the difference in praying to Mary and praying *with* Mary?

The difference is that Mary or any of the saints have no power on their own to answer prayers or perform miracles. Every good thing that a saint does or has done is a pure gift from God. God is so generous that He allows His faithful servants to participate in His work of salvation.

When we ask Mary and the saints to pray for us, we are asking that they would join us in prayer (just as I ask my friends to pray for me). But because the saints are already in heaven, they have a special closeness with the Lord, which makes their prayers more powerful. Scripture says that, "the eyes of the Lord are upon the righteous, and His ears are open to their prayer" (1 Peter 3:12). Who could be more righteous than the saints who are already enjoying total communion with God in heaven? So when we appeal to the Blessed Mother's (or any of the saints') intercession, we are simply asking our heavenly brothers and sisters to join us in prayer. "Where two or three are gathered in my name, there am I in their midst" (Matthew 18:20).

Is it wrong to wear a Rosary as a necklace or hang it in the rear view mirror?

Before we can talk about the rightness or wrongness of an action, we need to look at the item's purpose. A person could ask, "Is it wrong to use a wall clock as a paperweight?" We can see that while a clock could serve as a paperweight, its best function is to be hung on the wall in a way that displays the time. In a similar manner, while the Rosary can be worn around the neck or hung on the rear view mirror, the purpose of the Rosary is not to be a piece of jewelry or an item for decoration, but as a tool for meditation. The Rosary is a sacramental, which means it is a symbol of the graces that are given when one prays it. With that in mind, the Rosary needs to be honored as a prayerful and holy item. So is it ok to wear the Rosary as a necklace or hang it in the rear view mirror? As long as the Rosary is given the respect it deserves as a sacramental. The best place for a Rosary, however, is in your hands while on your knees.

We'd like to thank Sister Joseph Andrew for her contribution to this rosary resource. Sister is one of the foundresses of the Dominican Sisters of Mary, Mother of the Eucharist and she currently serves as the Vicaress and the Vocations Director.

The Dominican Sisters of Mary, Mother of the Eucharist is a Roman Catholic community of women religious based in Ann Arbor, Michigan. Their community was founded in the Dominican tradition to spread the witness of religious life in accord with Pope John Paul II's vision for a new evangelization.

Through profession of the vows of chastity, poverty, and obedience, along with a contemplative emphasis on Eucharistic adoration and Marian devotion, their community exists for the salvation of souls and the building of the Church throughout the world. As Dominicans, their primary apostolate is the education and formation of young people. They remain open to engaging the modern culture with new forms of evangelization in order to preach the Gospel and teach the Truth.

Dominican Sisters of Mary, Mother of the Eucharist
4597 Warren Road
Ann Arbor MI 48105
www.sistersofmary.org

LIFE
TEEN
®